THE COLLABORATION HACK

KIMBERLY & COACH CULBERTSON

THE COLLABORATION HACK

---

7 TOOLS OF TEAM DYNAMICS TO UPGRADE YOUR COMPANY CULTURE

K+C Business Books

STANDARD COPYRIGHT SHENANIGANS

or timeliness of the information contained in this book. The author and publisher disclaim all liability for any damages arising out of the use of the information contained in this book.

Please consult with an appropriate professional for specific legal or professional advice.

CONTENTS

CONTENTS

ACKNOWLEDGEMENTS

Lots of people to thank! Starting with you—we're so glad you're here!!

From Kimberly:

Ben and Jack, you are my favorite collaborators! You make every adventure better.

Mom and Dad, thanks for instilling in us the power of community and neighborhood.

Alan and Deb Hirsch, Tim Catchim, Rich Robinson, and Jessie Cruickshank, your ideas have shaped me and echo in the way we do community and into the content of this book. A big thanks to Kim Hammond and the Forge America crew, for instilling in me the idea that only practitioners should teach, and to the 5Q team, for deepening my imagination around collective intelligence.

Stacy Barton, your encouragement and listening ear helped me return to me. And also your writing is fantastic. It's so lovely to know you.

Barry and Robin, so grateful to work alongside you as you craft a culture that is truly good news.

Kimberly, for adventuring around the world and chasing all the moments—our collaboration always comes first!

Dad, Mom, and my extended family, especially Grandpa and Grandma Culbertson (owners of the Culbertson Roller Rink in Vandalia, Illinois), for teaching me the core elements of belonging, team dynamics, and love despite conflict—and that more transformation happens around the dinner table than can ever happen in the boardroom.

Our boy Jack, who puts up with all of our crazy running around and who (sometimes happily) gets dragged around to fun places like Miami for business engagements.

Aunt Elaine Culbertson, for teaching me to turn everything into a party.

Vera Baptist Church, for teaching me how to get up in front of a crowd and speak (with a suit coat on, of course, gotta have a speaking jacket ☺).

Dave Brumbaugh, for mentoring me into the tech industry 20+ years ago, and for walking with me through all the cray-cray of my college years.

Bill and Merilee Kulterman, for always being on my team.

Frost, Slammer, Nano, Hernandez, Charles, Delonte, Carmen, Carla, Tiny, Q, Jeremiah, Doughboy, Renee, The Twins, and all my Clemente kids for hanging tough out there! (Yes, I know you're all in your 30's now and some of you have kids of your own, but you'll always be my kids).

Adil, Shoiab, and Nash, for continuing to exemplify fantastic team dynamics.

From Both of Us:

Daughter Christa, Brian, and the 4 grandkids—Zeke, Ellie, Zakai, and Zayden—thank you for continuing to inspire us with your resiliency and hope. You bring us so much joy. We remain hopeful that you'll move to Texas someday, but until then we'll just keep visiting.

Abi Robins, we love every chance we have to work with you! Grateful to navigate the enneagram and the ups and downs of life with ya! Here's to yoga and climbing and biking and whatever we obsess about next.

Caleb and Olivia, thank you for being our best cheerleaders (and for keeping Cap when we have retreats at the house). So grateful to do this life as neighbors and friends. #BestCovidPodEver

Shelley Delayne, you created something wonderful and we're so glad we got to be a part of it. A huge thanks to the whole Orange Coworking crew—we took turns reminding each other that we were capable and that these dreams could work, and every one of those moments carried us through. The OG Orange Grove lives on and every time our paths cross, it brings us joy.

To our friends at Vox Veniae, who are bravely working toward a new paradigm of shared leadership in real time, y'all are the real deal. Wey, Christopher, Gena, and so many others, we could not be more grateful for you. Jonathan Shane, Sam, Liz, Melissa, Joe and Andrew, our Vox OGs, thank you for inviting us in and for walking alongside us in countless ways.

Joe Shannon from Newton Institute, thank you for deepening our capabilities through the MPACT platform.

Erica Payne Krause, from EP Photography, you're the best! Our height difference is no joke and has thwarted many a photographer—but not you! Grateful for how you always capture our energy, too.

Madison Adamson from Indie Eatz (Insta: @indie_eatz) and Chris Clarey (Insta: @cjclarey) from CH Hospitality, thank you for being our go-to private chefs for leadership retreats in Austin!

David Newman, Theresa French, Rina Mora, Allison Jokinen, Katie McCarthy, Ray Engan, and all our Do It! Marketing MBA team, thank you for believing in us and pushing us into a bigger, better business life! Shout-out to Cindy Skalicky and Jen Croneberger for continual inspiration! And special thanks to Larry Silverberg for encouragement and for pre-ordering the very first copy of this book before it was even finished!

Shelley Sperry, book coach extraordinaire, thanks for helping us sharpen up these chapters in such a tight timeframe!

And once again, to you dear reader, thanks for picking up this book ☺ Cheers to creating environments where people can thrive!

INTRODUCTION: WHY EVERY WORKPLACE NEEDS A LANGUAGE OF VALUE

We've all been there—a whisper across a breakroom table or a cubicle wall. "I can't believe he did that. What a jerk. I would never…"

You may be thinking even now about someone who irritates you—maybe it's their cloying, manipulative timidness, or, conversely, their sheer audacity. Or maybe you are sighing because what's coming to mind is a memory of someone who pulled your words or actions out of context, taking offense where you meant none.

As leadership, team dynamics, and culture consultants, we're all too familiar with this kind of conversation.

Nothing sinks collaboration, productivity, and creativity quite as quickly as a team that's spending its best energy fighting one another.

We're often called in to handle dire circumstances when managers have thrown up their hands, wondering if the only way back to good is to fire everyone and start fresh. But this is an incredibly expensive solution, both financially and in terms of your work culture, so we generally counsel companies to avoid it. That's why one of our unofficial mottos is:

We'll help you get the best results out of the team you already have.

While we do a lot of work with clients who want to set the stage for a healthy work culture, more often than not, we're walking into a mess. We see A LOT of conflict in this job. It's common for the person explaining the conflict to characterize the colleague in question as an evil mastermind, an insufferable brown-noser, or some other bleepity-bleep. Choose your own character assassination phrase—we've heard them all. But in reality, conflict rarely has its roots in the actions or words of one malicious person. Yes, you might have a truly evil coworker, but it's unlikely.

The problem is that our human default mode is to villainize, or at least distrust, people who are different from us. So, when we tell a coworker, "I would never have said that thing that way—what a [fill-in-the-blank]," we're making the subtle assertion that *our* way is the only right way. And if the person to whom we're venting thinks and feels like we do, it's easy for us to high-five and agree that we're right and all those other people are wrong.

Cut from the Same Cloth: Hiring an Army of Clones

That feeling of agreement—that these are *my people*, that we're the good guys, and they're the bad guys—is baked into the way we think. It has helped us team up to battle predators and survive for millennia. In positive terms, we call it *chemistry* or talk about being in sync and on the same wavelength as our friends and colleagues. But on the flip side, when we talk about our enemies living on another planet, casting them as impossible to understand or less than human, we get into trouble.

In the 21st century, few of us live out in the wild, battling lions, tigers, and bears on a daily basis. We live in a new age that requires collaboration, innovation, and creativity for survival, and our default Us-versus-Them setting leads to all kinds of problems, from sharing a not-so-covert eye roll across a boardroom table to declarations of war between nations. Globally, it fuels racism, sexism... really all the -isms.

In the workplace, what we see time after time is that the good feelings we associate with defaulting to the Us-versus-Them point of view lead to specific problems:

First, we see leaders hiring only people with whom they feel a resonance or a bond. They then train through example, consciously or accidentally, cloning a Mini-Me[1].

You've probably heard a boss or colleague say, "If I just had six of me, that would be perfect." And perhaps you've said something similar to a coworker?

Even if you don't realize it, the subtext of this phrase is that their way is the best, and no one else does it quite as well. It's pretty disrespectful to any coworkers being pushed aside in this fantasy scenario.

But beyond the inherent disrespect, let's pause to examine this phrase more closely:

If we really could create a team of six clones, we'd have twelve more hands, but still just one brain (essentially). No additional perspective. No increase in intelligence. Every person on this seven-person dream team would have the same weaknesses and blind spots.

Imagine a bodybuilder who aggressively works only one arm every day. Not only would they eventually look a bit wonky, but they'd have to deal with bigger problems over time. The weight of the strengthened muscles would pull on the rest of the body, causing pain. There would be an imbalance: They might have a strong handshake but get winded on the first flight of stairs. The pull of their stronger arm across their shoulders would likely result in a literal pain in the neck.

What we're looking for when we hire people like ourselves generally falls somewhere between easy agreement and a full-blown robot army. When someone challenges the leader of this type of team, it's considered an act of disloyalty. The challenger is accused of "not knowing their place."

Ultimately, this kind of leader just wants a team that fully supports his or her ideas, not a team that makes those ideas better.

When we hire for sameness, we are hiring for reduced intelligence.

The Symphony: Hiring a Team with Complementary Gifts

Do you know—or can you take a guess—How many symphonies have been written for only 100 flutes? Exactly zero[2]. Because no one wants to hear 100 flutes. The power of a symphony is in all the different instruments, each contributing their unique sounds but playing together. Drums, strings, saxophones, basses, horns a-plenty, all join in to achieve an emotional effect on the audience, an effect that one instrument alone simply couldn't create.

When we hire for diverse perspectives, we are hiring a symphony and increasing our team intelligence. This kind of team is always better than the sum of its parts. With more varied experiences, viewpoints, and preferences, this team can see the bigger picture, think creatively, and innovate in surprising ways. And if the team is also highly engaged and has overlapping gifts, they can make productivity skyrocket, plan for challenges, think strategically, and create the ongoing, positive results every manager dreams about. At least, they can do all this when their differences are respected and even appreciated.

I know what you're thinking: This is going to be hard.

And you're right.

Creating a culture of diversity of perspective takes some work. It requires fighting that default appreciation for sameness. And while this *can* happen organically (for example, in a team whose outlier saves their bacon at the last minute), it's better and easier when it's done with intentionality.

To help organizations all over the world find their way intentionally to a culture of diversity, we've come up with an approach we call the Collaboration Hack.

The Collaboration Hack

Every workplace needs a surefire way to increase team intelligence—to help all the players become a symphony.

After years of working with teams from dozens of diverse organizations, we've discovered that the solution is to cultivate a **Language of Value.**

At Kimberly & Coach, we know there are a lot of tools available to help organizations find the right language and license to describe how each person on their team is wired for collaboration, from the ubiquitous DISC assessment to the Harry Potter Sorting Hat[3]. We specialize in using an array of tools, including MPACT, CliftonStrengths, Myers-Briggs, and Enneagram[4].

When we are hired to work with teams, we almost always start with one of these tools. Once we've talked through the options and chosen the best tool for the team, we coach employees around their results and establish a team map. These actions install a specific Language of Value, or LOV, into the workplace culture.

When the LOV is in place:

- Each employee has the language and license to articulate their own preferences, talents, and perspectives.
- Each manager has data about how each team member will work best, where they'll need support, and how they'll feel appreciated.
- Each team member also has *neutral and positive language* for discussing differences. This helps a team move beyond character assassination and villainizing one another to expressing real value and appreciation: *This person is different from me, and that is a gift.*

Together, we have set the stage for a brand-new paradigm. With an established Language of Value, we can begin to invite the full intelligence and engagement of our teams. From there, we can hear the symphony tuning up and the future looks so much better than before!

What's Coming Up in This Book

In the chapters that follow, we'll talk more about building a vocabulary around how differences are gifts, not problems. We'll show you some of our proven LOV tools that enable organizations to identify preferences and talents. We'll reveal how we've helped team members and management start talking about exactly what each person needs to do great work. And, if you're wondering which tool mentioned above might be right for your team, you can find our favorite Languages of Value and a Choose-Your-Tool Worksheet in the Appendices at the end.

Now, let's go!

REFLECT

1. What stands out to you from this chapter?

REFLECT

2. How will you put this into action to improve your own collaboration skills?

REFLECT

3. How will you utilize this with your team, family, or community?

ADDITIONAL NOTES

SCAFFOLDING FOR BRILLIANCE

In 2022, the Metropolitan Transit Authority of New York dumped over 1000 subway cars into the Atlantic Ocean to create the scaffolding for artificial reefs[5]. Before you start a firestorm of backlash about the environmental impact, and why this was just a cheap way to scrap old subway cars, please note that artificial coral reefs have been used since the 17th century to provide a structure on which coral can grow and thrive. Artificial reefs are valuable footholds for coral, which help rebuild marine ecosystems and bring more life to an area of the ocean that might have previously been barren. More coral helps increase the biodiversity of an area, creating a better habitat for fish—and fish, in turn, help feed somewhere around three billion people[6] around the world.

No big deal, right? One innovative, well-thought-out action—putting old subway cars in a struggling marine habitat—creates a cascade of positive changes, large and small.

Implementing a Language of Value, or LOV, in a workplace can have a similar cascading effect. Coral is surrounded by a particular ocean habitat, just like every shop has a workplace culture surrounding its team. The question is: Is it the culture that the company actually wants? Is it creating the results companies rave about? Is it a habitat where people thrive?

Regardless of the context, culture is essentially a shared habitat made up of stories, rituals, food and drink, clothing, ways of relating, and what we mourn and celebrate. As human beings, we look for ways to connect, and culture sets the stage for those connections.

When we talk about culture in the workplace, a lot of people think only of events that honor nationality, ethnicity, or heritage. These events are certainly part of culture, but every company or organization also has its own distinctive workplace culture, complete with shared stories, traditions, and expectations.

When it's done with intention, a Language of Value can become a powerful shared element of the workplace culture and the start of something good.

Regardless of which LOV you choose— MPACT, Myers-Briggs, CliftonStrengths, Enneagram, DISC, Working Genius, whatever[7]—any of them serve a similar purpose and help your organization scaffold for diversity. When we drop a Language of Value into the waters of workplace culture, **it provides an intentional "reef" that conversations and relational patterns can grow around.**

Word to the Wise

Before we get into this topic too deeply, there's something we need to be cautious about. Please keep in mind that assessment tools can be misused and abused. Instead of using the tools to help people understand each other's preferences and styles of working, they are sometimes used as executive evaluative tools to sort, compartmentalize, limit, and restrict. That's *not* the right way to use these tools.

We're looking to build a work culture around a Language of Value, not a Language of Limitation.

We've watched leaders use these tools to stereotype and disqualify people, and when that happens, they not only get negative results, but can also end up inoculating people against the good aspects of the tools. So be careful as you implement!

A Scaffold You Can Build On

When kept in the right context and used well, LOV tools can provide everyone on a team with a vocabulary to understand why we need each other. One of our favorite tools, the MPACT assessment, uses this idea as a primary pillar:

What you are good at and like and see isn't always what I'm good at and like and see, and that's valuable.

If we buy into the idea that everyone is basically the same, we put blinders on our teams, which can lead us straight into a huge dumpster fire that could have been avoided. And when that fire ignites, someone in the back of the room will chime in, "I knew that would happen," as they stare at the proverbial charred remains with disdain.

But the folks in charge didn't know what was happening, because they never opened their ears enough to listen to a perspective that was different from their own. And the wiser people in the room didn't try to speak up, because they knew the leaders didn't like conflict and that in their workplace culture, disagreement equaled disrespect.

But when we simply change what we're talking about in a workplace, we can begin to see what we've been missing. Conversations around Languages of Value can provide the scaffolding for brilliance and keep us out of a jam. That's because vocabulary builds neural pathways[8], and around those neural pathways we get more capability. We not only become more open to other things that exist outside of our own unique vision, but people become more empathetic as well. Access to diverse perspectives can help a shop look at an issue from different angles and get a clearer picture of dangers and benefits.

When Satya Nadella took over Microsoft, he brought in the value and language of empathy for the customer, not as a nice-to-have extra, but as an innovation engine[9]. That new core value has helped to bring Microsoft to a trillion-dollar valuation. Instead of the traditional my-way-or-the-highway attitude we've seen so often in the C-Suite, Nadella partnered with long-time competitors like Apple and Google to further enhance Microsoft's portfolio of services and in turn, enhanced the value that the partners bring to customers. Simply put, Nadella re-centered the organization with a new vocabulary, and in doing so, created new capabilities and built new value throughout the team.

A strong, embedded LOV can help tear down the silos of hubris and dictatorial management that make for a terrible work environment, bringing more connection and partnership within a team and across teams. LOVs not only help us to mediate conflict more quickly, but they can also short-circuit conflict before it even starts, since teammates now have a neutral vocabulary for a diversity of perspectives. We have seen this happen time and time again in our work, even in relationally challenging industries like construction.

"You're such a bleepity-bleep," becomes wildly more respectful after a Language of Value is embedded. It might sound something more like, "I know you prefer to move quickly, but I'd really like to slow down enough to evaluate the risk here."

Easy Peasy, Right?

So, all we have to do is have our employees take an assessment, and that will solve all our problems?

Yeah, don't we all wish? But, of course, there's more to it.

Let's jump back to the subway cars used to scaffold artificial reefs. The first time they used the technique in 2001 was very successful. The MTA lowered a set of Red-bird subway cars into the Atlantic off the East Coast[10]. The cars were made of carbon steel and created a gorgeous reef that increased the amount of marine food by 400 times over 7 years. Unfortunately, a more recent dump of subway cars was less successful. These Bright-liner cars were made of spot-welded stainless steel, and the ocean currents immediately started ripping them apart.

Our point is that the right tool in the right place is important. Just like with the subway cars, some tools will work better than others, depending on the currents of culture. Data-driven tools like MPACT and Clifton-Strengths can be great in shops where trust is low and more positive language is needed. Enneagram, on the other hand, is a narrative-based tool that can help individuals manage their reactivity and shine in their gifting, especially in smaller teams where trust is high.

Even when a company has chosen the best tool for their needs, though, a one-and-done approach isn't that helpful. There's an old leadership adage, "Vision leaks." Adding more details and reinforcement of your organization's principles over time reinforces and improves your scaffolding. Many companies have value plaques on the wall as reminders and vision documents of dozens and even hundreds of pages that sit on a shelf[11].

We think it's great to define your values and vision well, just like it's important to choose and implement a Language of Value in the first place. But this becomes an exercise in futility until the Vision, Values, and Language of Value are thoroughly integrated into conversations, company meetings, mediation sessions, trainings, and other communications. This will ensure that these empathy-building tools become second nature, rather than an interruption.

Things to Remember:

- Languages of Value can provide a **scaffolding for brilliance and culture to grow around,** just like subway cars in an artificial reef, and can help workplace culture grow into a healthier space.
- Choosing the right LOV for your workplace

environment is important, just like choosing the right starter material for an artificial reef.

- Integrating a Language of Value into the everyday operations of your shop can provide long-term benefits and a starting place for more conversations, best practices, and cultural patterns to grow around.
- Languages of Value should not be used for evaluation or review. They should be used as shared tools to help provide empathy, understanding, and connection among team members to increase team intelligence, not competition.

REFLECT

1. What stands out to you from this chapter?

REFLECT

2. How will you put this into action to improve your own collaboration skills?

REFLECT

3. How will you utilize this with your team, family, or community?

ADDITIONAL NOTES

| 28 |

OUT OF THE ECHO CHAMBER, INTO THE TENSION

If embedding a Language of Value and appreciation for diversity is so great, why doesn't every company do it?

This is a fair question, and there are a number of answers, like the tried and true, *We've Never Done It That Way* ™ and the omnipresent, *We'll Get to It When Things Slow Down*™. But, by far, we get the most opposition from leaders who fear *discomfort.* In this chapter, we'll talk about how to overcome and even embrace that discomfort.

The Echo Chamber

Few things can make you feel as smart and safe and comfy as an echo chamber. *See,* it says to you, *your way is the only right way. Here are ten people who agree*[12]! Unfortunately, nothing puts you and your team at risk quite as much as an echo chamber, because no one in there can warn you about impending potholes or suggest a better path.

Executives love to hear they're right, and they love to get their own way. We hear it all the time, especially the higher up the executive ladder a leader is:

"Everything just goes smoother and faster when people do what I say. If I invite everyone's opinions, we'll never get anything done."

Well, that's not entirely true. It's easy to miss the downside of efficiently getting your way every time. Slowing down to invite, digest, and act on the intelligence of your team does take time, especially when doing so is new. But the time you invest here will lead to better decision-making, higher engagement, and improved productivity down the road.

And of course, high-level leaders who do the work to shift this paradigm and invite a fully-engaged team to share their full perspective with them will face a second obstacle: Sooner or later, the leaders will come up against the real discomfort of being challenged, especially by people below them.

If you've heard a manager say, "Who do you think

you are?" or "He's getting a little big for his britches," then chances are, you've seen this struggle firsthand.

But the cost of retreating into the echo chamber is high.

Gallup completes a survey regularly[13] which rates whether employees are engaged (participating fully to the best of their ability), disengaged (giving partial effort or doing the bare minimum to continue to be employed), or actively disengaged (consciously sabotaging their company's efforts in little or big ways). Consistently, only about 30 percent of respondents rate as engaged, and around 20 percent are actively disengaged.

These are terrible stats if you're paying a staff; it means seven out of ten people are not giving their best effort, and two of them are working against you!

It's easy to read these stats with judgement:

No one wants to work hard anymore. This generation is so entitled; they just want everything to be handed to them.

But when researchers follow up with that 70 percent about why they aren't engaged at work, the most common answer might surprise you. They most often report that their supervisors don't want their opinion or participation. Their full engagement has been slapped back, so now they keep their head down and collect their paycheck.

Chances are, you've heard a version of this slapback more often than you realize:

"Just go do your job, and I'll do mine."

"If I want your opinion, I'll ask for it."
"I don't pay you to think."
Oof[14].

A More Intelligent Culture

Here's the good news. We can get comfortable with tension and conflict. When we've got a Language of Value in our workplace culture, we've got a framework for *productive conflict,* and higher levels of respect, even in conflict. An LOV can become a force for dismantling the echo chamber, leaving a new structure in its place.

With this paradigm in place, we move away from saying, "Conflict is bad" to arguing that "Conflict is intelligence at work." This can make all the difference. We also begin to build up our tolerance for disagreement, and as we do that, we can more authentically welcome divergent thinking. Rather than retreating from differences of perspective, we can lean in and get curious. And when we do this, we suck the marrow out of conflict. Rather than rolling eyes and calling names, we can say, "I'm not seeing it that way—tell me more."

Teams that have built this conflict-positive framework into the fabric of their decision-making cultures often *look forward* to disagreement. We've been in the rooms where this happens, and it's more like friendly banter than the vicious infighting for which so many of us have unfortunately built up a tolerance. What a waste of energy!

High-performing teams know how vital an authentic feedback loop is, so they actually request it as part of their process. They say, "Okay, here's my idea, now poke your holes. What am I not seeing?" And because team members know they can handle disagreement without taking it personally, they are less afraid to speak their minds. The process is far more enjoyable and results in better, more confident decision-making.

In the next four chapters of this book, we'll share key concepts that will help you arrive at a place where team members want to speak up. These Tools for Tension will help you create the best possible collaborative environment. And each time you use them, you'll be building a ladder for those disengaged team members to climb until they too are bringing their full intelligence to work.

Things to Remember:

- When you invite additional intelligence, you may also get additional conflict.
- Conflict can bring out new perspectives when team members feel safe to disagree.
- Getting curious (rather than judgmental) can help to disarm a conflict episode so that additional intelligence can be revealed.

REFLECT

1. What stands out to you from this chapter?

REFLECT

2. How will you put this into action to improve your own collaboration skills?

REFLECT

3. How will you utilize this with your team, family, or community?

ADDITIONAL NOTES

| 37 |

CHAPTER

4

TWO TYPES OF CONFLICT

Every business has a mission. The team breaks the mission into targets, and every team member has an approach to hitting their targets (and yes, you can use the terms KPI, goal, objective, milestone—whatever terms your last management seminar taught you). So when we encounter conflict, we first want to ask, which kind of conflict is this: target or approach?

Target Conflicts

A Target Conflict happens when two or more people are going after different targets or goals. Take a look at one example:

Rajesh works in business development at a manufac-

that they can focus on coding the functionality that's unique to the project. Eduardo feels that taking the time to write a new library will give the company flexibility to write exactly what's needed and also provide another product the company could license out to other software development firms.

Eduardo and Jamie have two different approaches but the same target.

Okay, What's Next?

In these two scenarios, are any of these team members evil or morally wrong?

Nope.

Each of the hypothetical team members, who are based on real people we've worked with, are simply operating from their own perspectives. And in each scenario, the first step in resolving the conflicts is to determine what kind of conflict the team members are actually having.

Rajesh and Sammy aren't in alignment on the target they're trying to hit. Eduardo and Jamie aren't in alignment about their approach to the same target.

When tempers flare and people on your team become passionate about their particular target or approach—especially when it affects bonuses, continued employment, or profitability—they can become triggered by fear or past experiences. If that happens, solutions become more difficult to uncover due to name-calling, accusations, and other emotional lashing out.

In the next few chapters, we'll tackle ways to start de-escalating both kinds of conflicts, but it's important to remember that in most situations the people in conflict are not evil or driven by bad intentions, even though we may not agree with their approaches or understand what they are trying to achieve.

At this point, a lot of folks we work with like to ask, "What about morality?"

We tell them that's a target issue. Moral imperatives are usually different targets.

We've also heard things like, "I just don't like that person."

That's an approach issue. Personality conflicts are a flavor of Approach Conflicts.

And one of our favorite responses is: "I would never do it *that* way."

Well, yes, that's an approach issue as well. And of course, you wouldn't go about solving an issue the same way the other person would. You are different people, and you see things differently because your experiences, neurology, and preferences are all different.

While sometimes a situation does get to a point where lawyers, guns, and money become necessary (as songwriter Warren Zevon says[15]), most conflicts don't need to escalate to that level, especially in the workplace.

To unravel a conflict to a point where resolution becomes possible, we first have to understand what

kind of conflict is actually occurring because it's tremendously helpful as we begin to work toward a solution. Trying to solve a target problem with an approach solution will never work and vice versa.

And, of course, there are times when we have both kinds of conflict happening in an episode. Often, the team members involved in the conflict have no idea what's going on; they only know they're angry about a *thing*. Using these two categories of Target Conflicts and Approach Conflicts can provide grounding and a concreteness to the situation that helps us stay on track toward resolution.

When the Issues Go Beyond Targets and Approaches

Sometimes a conflict actually does involve actual evil, or at least malicious individuals. We can debate the definition of evil all day long, but instances of criminal activity, physical harm or threats of physical harm, stalking, sabotage, policy and safety infractions, and similar issues need to be dealt with appropriately. That may mean working with law enforcement agencies and lawyers as necessary.

When issues of mental health arise as part of a team conflict, that's an entirely different topic, too. It's important to work with your HR representative

---

> to figure out how best to support those individuals and minimize fallout and negative effects on workplace culture.
>
> These kinds of issues, which go beyond Target and Approach Conflicts, are outside the scope of this book. Leaders should plan ahead to determine what the organization's responses might be and how leaders will know when escalation and outside help are necessary. Consult your local HR representative, law enforcement agency, and legal counsel for help.

Now that we've got the types of conflict down, we can get smart about how we're processing conflict. And as we do so, we'll pull back the curtain and find the inherent intelligence. Fun!

Things to Remember:

- Almost all workplace conflicts come down to either Target or Approach Conflicts.
- A **Target Conflict** is when two or more people are chasing after different goals.
- An **Approach Conflict** is when two or more people are going after the same goal but are approaching it from different perspectives.
- The first step in resolving a workplace conflict is uncovering what kind of conflict is occurring.

REFLECT

1. What stands out to you from this chapter?

REFLECT

2. How will you put this into action to improve your own collaboration skills?

REFLECT

3. How will you utilize this with your team, family, or community?

ADDITIONAL NOTES

GUARDING AND GROWING

Imagine you're part of a community garden. In fact, you're the leader of the project. You've got a huge space next to a park, and your mission is to benefit the neighborhood. You've gathered a team of volunteers who are passionate about gardening in order to discuss plans for the space.

You may think gardeners are all incredibly grounded and kind, but there are some big personalities in this group, and they've got strong opinions about what the neighborhood needs. Before you know it, the conversation gets heated, and you're wondering what you've gotten yourself into.

Half of the group wants a gorgeous space that inspires

contemplation and joy. Pathways, benches, butterflies, a grassy knoll for picnics—the whole shebang.

"We're surrounded by concrete and strip malls," they say. "This garden can provide a reprieve!"

It sounds wonderful, right? If we could portal there right now, we just might.

Unfortunately, this meeting is not that peaceful, because just as you were imagining your picnic under the shade tree, one of your neighbors just stood up and said, "How selfish and entitled can you be?! What a crock. I thought we were trying to help people."

You see, he knows that this neighborhood is in a food desert[16], and he's come to the meeting with one goal: to make sure every neighbor has more access to fruits and vegetables. He thinks a "decorative park" is entirely missing the point.

In response, a neighbor from the first group stands and screams at you, "I didn't realize you had to be a bleeding-heart liberal to be part of this committee!"

Hoo boy. How do you get this train back on the rails?

First, you explain that the discussion has to move away from character assassination. "We have different targets here, but that doesn't mean we can call each other 'selfish and entitled' or 'bleeding-heart liberals.'"

Second, it's time to get curious and start asking better questions.

Guarding and Growing

When we find ourselves in any conflict, two of the best questions we can ask are:

- What are you trying to grow here?
- What are you guarding against here?

It's easy to see the answers in the example above: One neighbor is trying to grow beauty, and the other is trying to grow food, right? As is often the case, they feel they are on separate sides, but that's rarely completely true. Both agree that a garden can help their neighbors, but they disagree about what kind of help to prioritize.

We can also dig into what each person is guarding against. This is often when we see emotional reactivity take off. The gardener who wants to feed his neighbors wants to guard against predators that would steal into the garden and eat the food, so he's arguing for a tall wall around the garden. The gardener who wants beauty wants to guard the view, so she doesn't want a wall at all.

In reality, the two goals—beauty and sustenance— aren't mutually exclusive. If we lay down our arms, we can often find a more intelligent solution, something that will be better than either option would be on its own.

We need to think "both-and" instead of "either-or[17]" whenever possible.

When we get *curious* about what our opponent is guarding and growing, we automatically inject some empathy into a conversation. Instead of trying to win an argument, I'm seeking to understand. And when I do that, I may realize there's some validity to their point of view.

Once we can see the other person's side, we are far more likely to work together to create a solution that honors both of the needs being expressed. If we agree the neighborhood in our example can benefit from both more color and more nutrients, we can start to find solutions that will get us there.

Perhaps we could grow food at the center of our garden and surround it with pathways and gorgeous, colorful flowers. Neighbors passing by would be able to drink in the color, but a tasteful fence would provide a barrier against rabbits and deer that might want to snack on the vegetables. Maybe we aren't using as much space for grassy knolls, but instead, we include picnic tables for families to enjoy.

Suddenly, we're on the same team and everyone wins.

Outside the Garden

This metaphor works well in the garden, of course. But we see it work just as well all the time in corporate and relational spaces.

The creative team at a restaurant chain wants to go big on a rebrand. They're looking to grow impact and brand loyalty, and they're guarding against fading into the background in their industry. But the finance department is guarding against overspending and looking to grow a more comfortable margin before taking on another big risk.

Do all members of the team want to stay relevant *and* make sure every employee gets a paycheck next quarter? Then it's important for everyone to work together toward both goals. That may mean the creative team scales back their plans, and the finance team meets them somewhere in the middle. Or it may mean they postpone the rebrand, but schedule it as a priority for the following year, setting some money aside over the next two quarters to reduce the risk.

In another scenario, a nonprofit food aid organization has received a large donation. The executive director is arguing for an improvement in infrastructure to make the group's work more efficient. This will save money in the long run and increase the amount they can distribute over time. Her board of directors wants to grow the immediate impact of the donation by using it to provide more services now. They're guarding against the perception that this nonprofit doesn't distribute enough of its donations.

Perhaps the executive director needs to listen more fully to the board so that she can move forward in two key ways: First, she will spend time showing a clear link between improved infrastructure and their ability to provide more services long-term. Second, the board will help its director communicate carefully so that their key donors know why the funds are being spent this way.

Even though she still chooses to proceed in the direction she originally proposed, the executive director can now do so with more intelligence and finesse, totally aware of the landmines buried in this allocation.

Wherever your disagreement lies, guarding and growing is a tool you'll want in your kit. Once we move out of the Us-versus-Them framework and unite around our common mission, we can move forward with respect and come up with intelligent solutions that take every team member's perspective into account.

Things to Remember:

- Everyone has priorities they are actively trying to grow and threats they are guarding against.
- Most of the time, these priorities and threats are not spoken.
- Conflicts can often be broken down by identifying what each individual is growing and guarding against.
- Examining priorities and threats can sometimes lead to conflict resolution by finding solutions that incorporate multiple priorities and multiple preventative solutions. This happens when we think in a "both-and" fashion instead of in terms of "either-or."

REFLECT

1. What stands out to you from this chapter?

REFLECT

2. How will you put this into action to improve your own collaboration skills?

REFLECT

3. How will you utilize this with your team, family, or community?

ADDITIONAL NOTES

FIT-SPLIT-CONTEND-TRANSCEND

Once we understand the kind of conflict team members may be having (or are about to have) and identify what they may be guarding or growing, it's time to sit down and hash out a resolution.

Conflict comes and goes in episodes, and to bring a conflict episode to resolution, the participants often must come to the table. All conflicts do come to a resolution at some point, so take heart that your conflict won't last forever.

Before you get too excited about this, though, we want to step back for just a minute and look at something that a lot of folks ignore:

Conflict can be an engine for increasing intelligence, connection, and collaboration on your team.

No, really. We're serious. Stop laughing.

Okay, fine, go ahead and laugh. Just get it out of your system.

We good? Let's roll on.

We've seen it happen over and over and even experienced it ourselves as husband and wife. Conflict uncovers what's happening behind the smiles and fake corporate masks. When handled well, the benefits of engaging in conflict can be huge.

Let's get down to how we can walk through a conflict resolution session with the goal of increasing intelligence, connection, and collaboration in mind. This framework can help us navigate a raging conflict, or it can set the stage for healthy debate, especially in environments in which team members are hesitant to voice competing viewpoints for fear of conflict.

A Framework for Intelligent Debate

In the book *Managing on the Edge*, author Richard Tanner Pascale proposes a framework that he says will transform companies by harnessing conflict. It's called, *Fit-Split-Contend-Transcend.* Pascale uses the framework primarily for restructuring giant corporations, and we have adapted it to use in smaller-scale decision-making and conflict-resolution conversations.

In our team dynamics and workplace culture consulting, we've used this adapted framework with companies of all shapes and sizes, from nonprofits to small businesses to large corporations. It's extremely helpful because it creates a container for harnessing the intelligence on any given team. Our friend Rich Robinson calls this "Scenius," or the genius on the scene. We want to tap into that collective intelligence, but we want to do it in a way that doesn't take forever and doesn't turn friends into enemies.

This fantastic framework often brings about unanimous decisions. But as you know, unanimous agreement is not always possible. So, in workplace environments, it's important that the group knows, even before the conversation starts, who will make the final call, if needed. That person will benefit from this process tremendously, because when that time comes, they'll have a full picture and a greater ability to make the right call.

Phase 1: Fit

In the Fit stage, we build a foundation for unity. Before we dig into the conflict or decision-making, we want to establish where team members are already in alignment. We can start with the mission of the company as an initial shared understanding, and then see if we're in agreement with a general direction or target for the current project or question on the table.

We cannot tell you how many times we've watched leaders bypass this phase and rush their teams toward conflict. They don't mean any harm; they just don't want to slow down to make sure people are all on the same page first. They understand what the company is trying to do, and they assume the room is full of agreement. But trust us—*don't skip this phase.*

We *want* to figure out what unifies us as team members, because we are about to court disagreement on purpose! We need a strong foundation of unity before we do this so that it will frame the way we debate the ideas. By doing this, we remind people in the conversation that we are all in this together, looking for the win-win that will best serve our purposes.

Remember our conversation about Target Conflict and Approach Conflict from Chapter 4? You'll see this come into play right from the start.

If team members are aiming for different targets, that often becomes apparent when we take time for the Fit phase. It's important to work toward target agreement now so that we are unified on where we are headed together in this decision-making process.

On the other hand, team members are often already in agreement about what they're trying to collaborate on, but they have different ideas about how to get there. This kind of Approach Conflict is more likely to surface in Phase 2, so the Fit phase is quick and easy.

Once the initial agreement has been established, once we're clear on how we all FIT together and that we're all on the same team, we can move on to Phase 2.

> *Pro Tips*
>
> **When conflict is already simmering, taking a moment to categorize the existing conflict as either Target or Approach can set you up for a win right from the start.** This simple categorization often begins to defuse some of the more contentious energy in the room. The *Thing We're Fighting About*™ starts to become more concrete and in focus.
>
> **During mediation sessions, we often refer to the Language of Value if one has been selected and implemented as we establish unity.** This provides some neutral language and grounding and reminds participants that we value differences in perspective and approach. Using a Team Map with the team members' profiles from the LOV can also help keep the conversation relaxed because it's something that's shared by everyone that we can refer to in moments of tension.

Phase 2: Split

In the Split phase, we seek out the spaces where we disagree. We try to get every perspective on the table. We're not arguing about what is *right* just yet—we'll get there in Phase 3. For now, we are looking around and asking: "What do we notice?" "What perspectives do we have in the room?"

More facets of the diamond will be surfaced, and often we uncover information that makes at least one of the participants say, "Hmmmmm…" Kind of like Arsenio Hall and C+C Music Factory back in the 1990s[18].

But *how* do we get all those perspectives on the table? We've been to many a meeting where everyone is silent and agreeable in the room, and then they each voice their opposition in the hallway in "the meeting after the meeting" (If you're wondering, this is rarely helpful).

If we are in a conversation that we want to begin and end on the same day, such as a goal-setting session at an executive team retreat or a mediation of conflict between two employees, then we'll want to do the split intentionally during that session.

We'll grab sticky notes if we want a colorful wall of options, or we'll just speak about the options in the group while one person captures ideas and priorities on a whiteboard or in a notebook. We want all the perspectives we can generate within whatever time frame is available to us.

However, we often have a decision to make or a conflict to solve that's going to take research, data, or contemplation. The people in the room for Phase 1 often need to check in with their teams before they bring ideas forward. In this kind of situation, we spread the process over many meetings: First, the team will meet for the Fit conversation, making sure they're all on the same page. The participants will then break for a designated amount of time to do research and gather input. They'll reconvene for the Split phase, sharing the perspectives they've gathered.

Especially when people are new to the process, people often come into the conversation with one opinion. If you're facilitating this phase, consider asking, "Are there other options?" or "Is there a third way?" or "We've got the obvious ideas on the board, what's the craziest solution you can think of?" Push your team to look around the proverbial room at what they're not seeing or not considering.

When we're innovating around strategy or trying to solve a problem, the Split conversation is often a lot of fun. But when we're using this method to address conflict, it can be a bit harder. Here the Split Phase gives us a chance to take the conflict out of ourselves as much as possible and "set it on the table," if you will. We often encourage the team members to look at the conflict from as many angles as possible. In cases of conflict, it can be helpful to bring in some empathy questions, like, "How do you think David experienced that moment?" or "What do you feel if you put yourself in his shoes?"

During the Split Phase, we often see lightbulbs go on for people as they realize the value other perspectives can bring.

> **Pro Tip:**
>
> **The key challenge in the Split Phase is to**

> **hold off on debating the validity of the ideas or arguing about what is most important.** A good facilitator will have to remind people that we are waiting to discuss the merits of the info on the table. Phase 2 is only about listening and capturing information. When people jump straight into arguments about the ideas, it almost always shuts down the Split flow, and that means you might not get to the *Really Good Idea*™.
>
> Don't let yourself get bullied into Phase 3 until you're ready!

Phase 3: Contend

In the Contend Phase, we're now ready to debate the ideas!

We're arguing for what we see as priorities. We're talking about the potholes we see in this particular path. We're countering a point in conflict with our own story or with evidence.

When we're ideating and looking for solutions, two easy initial questions are, "What ideas on the table rise to the top for you?" and "What ideas make you uncomfortable or worried?"

When we notice a lot of tension or enter the conversation to address a specific conflict, we'll want to start there. We may begin with a question like, "From what we've already expressed, what piece of this conflict do you feel you'd like to discuss more?" or "Now that we've put the conflict on the table, so to speak, what are you noticing about the perspective or feelings of the other person?"

If you skip the Fit Phase, you're more likely to get an answer like, "I'm noticing that my colleague is a selfish bleepity-bleep!" Super unhelpful. So, make it clear that this process requires openness, respect, and empathy in your Fit conversation and don't be afraid to call on that agreement throughout the process.

Pro Tip

Don't be afraid to take a break if the energy in the room becomes too antagonistic. Isolating the actual conflict or staying on track in the face of conflict can be challenging at times, especially when tempers flare.

When team members are in a heightened state of reactivity, we've seen huge benefits when we've paused to take a walk or decided to pick up the conversation after the individuals involved have "slept on it." This strategy almost always yields drastically better results than pushing through. When people's "lids are flipped," the conversation often becomes less productive, and the ROI on pushing through decreases exponentially.

Not sure if the participants need a break? Don't be afraid to ask them. Even if they choose to stay

> the course, asking the question is often a pattern interrupt that helps people re-regulate their emotions.

Phase 4: Transcend

In the Transcend Phase, we seek harmony between multiple perspectives. The goal isn't necessarily for one side or the other to "win," but rather to find peaceful resolution and to leverage any new insights that may have come from the conversation.

Once we've found common ground, figured out what kind of conflict we're experiencing, pushed the ideas around, and heard from every person, all the people in the room are always happy, and it's back to work singing the Smurf song[19]! Right?

Sometimes, yes. Minus the Smurf song, that is. Probably.

Often, the different perspectives can Voltron up, and even better solutions and innovations come from the conversation. In fact, the new revelations and epiphanies may not have been possible at all without the spark of the conflict.

But let's remember that we are not in La-La Land. Everyone involved in the decision-making conversation or conflict episode may not be happy with the outcome.

When a group gets to the Transcend Phase and doesn't come to a unanimous agreement, someone must make the final call. Throughout this process,

the designated person should be listening carefully and asking great questions, so that when push comes to shove, they can make the most educated, intelligent choice.

It's important that the whole team already knows who the final decision-maker will be. That way, we are not creating an expectation that just because someone has been invited to the table, they'll definitely get their way. I have sat across from way too many disgruntled team members who are asking some version of, "If they weren't going to listen to me, why did they even ask me? Why did they waste my time?"

By setting an expectation that a stalemate will lead us to put the final decision in one person's hands at the outset, we can short-circuit some negative thoughts, replacing them with the knowledge that all input is valued and important. However, you are not the only person in this room, and your input will be part, but not all, of the decision-making wisdom.

When this is done well, even when someone doesn't get their way, team members who have engaged in debate or conflict through this model are far more likely to feel that their concerns and perspectives have been heard and considered. They are also more likely to understand why a particular direction has been chosen, even if they don't love it. And because everyone in the group has heard their points, it's also far more likely that the "No" they've received could turn into a "Not yet."

> ### Pro Tip
>
> **This is a great place to use a decision-making framework like DACI[21]**, which clearly identifies the Driver (the person calling for the decision), the Approver (the person who can veto or approve the call), the Contributors (those whose input is needed), and the Informed (those who need to know about the decision).

An Important Caveat

This framework works quite well even when there's highly charged conflict to navigate because people tend to want the best for the organization and for each other. Fit-Split-Contend-Transcend helps create those positive outcomes. But what if the intent on either or both sides is malicious? What if one or both parties are intent on destroying the other?

Realistically, not every conflict can be resolved without the aforementioned lawyers, guns, and money (but skip the guns—this is corporate conflict we're talking about here, not a military operation—that's a whole different book).

In the case of a heated business conflict, team members may need to be set on a different path.

Yes, I mean fired. Sent packing. Invited to transition. Whatever term you want.

Sometimes team members may not choose or be able

to eliminate toxicity from the conflict, and one or both parties may need to be terminated. Sometimes that just sucks.

When this happens, we mourn and learn whatever lessons we can from the situation. We see a therapist if we need to, and then we move on to the next challenge that's screaming for our attention.

But that's not the *usual* outcome, so be encouraged. From our years of experience, if we're not dealing with someone bent on destruction, and the mission of the company is still a fit, resolution is generally possible. In fact, we've even seen team members who were practically at each other's throats later become friends and collaborate effectively, not just with one another but with other colleagues as well, for the betterment of the company and the team around them.

When we do this well, conflict doesn't derail us. It drives us toward something better! And that's always good news.

Things to Remember:

- Conflict isn't forever.
- A structured approach to conflict resolution can bring concrete steps to the conflict episode.
- Fit-Split-Contend-Transcend is a great framework for many, but not all, conflicts.
- Conflict can be beneficial if approached from the right perspective.

· Sometimes, you must fire toxic team members, and sometimes team members will choose to leave the organization.

REFLECT

1. What stands out to you from this chapter?

REFLECT

2. How will you put this into action to improve your own collaboration skills?

REFLECT

3. How will you utilize this with your team, family, or community?

ADDITIONAL NOTES

CONFLICT RESOLUTION STYLES

We usually try to practice what we preach in our business when we're at home with our son Jack, so here's a lesson about costs and benefits we've shared early and often with him:

You often have to choose between short-term benefits with long-term difficulty, or short-term difficulty with long-term benefits.

By now you've realized that if you ask for differences of perspective, you'll sometimes find yourself slogging through conflict. You've invited it. But the truth is, those short-term conflicts will bring you long-term benefits in the end. There are high costs for avoiding today's conflict: Not only will that conflict get bigger and messier later, when it's finally out in the open, but when you muffle the voices at the table to avoid short-term conflict, you lose out on creativity, intelligence, innovation, and stronger decision-making down the road.

We get it. Few people love conflict, but now you've got tools you can use to deal with it.

- You can determine if this conflict is a Target Conflict or an Approach Conflict (or both).
- You can reframe the Us-versus-Them standoff by getting curious about what people are guarding and growing.
- And you can use the Fit-Split-Contend-Transcend discussion framework to plan for and de-villainize conflict.

In the end, we're just a consulting duo, standing in front of a reader, asking you to consider a short-term challenge on behalf of those long-term benefits.

If you're not quite convinced by now, you're probably thinking about the elephant in the room:

In the heat of the moment, the best of us can accidentally cause harm—and if we're honest, sometimes we're mad enough to do it on purpose.

When disagreements turn into reactivity and character assassination, it just doesn't feel good. When this happens, the solution is not to shrink away like a dog with its tail between its legs and swear off tension and debate once and for all. At least, we hope you won't. You can always take a short break to manage your reactivity, but then it will be time to repair the harm done in the conflict.

And as we've said and demonstrated many times in these pages: *People are complex, and we are all different.* So, it won't surprise you when we share that what helps one person find their way back to good will not necessarily work for the next person. And that brings us to the topic of Conflict Resolution Styles.

Three Pathways for Resolving Conflict

We first came across the Conflict Resolution Styles in our study of the Enneagram. But whether or not you're using Enneagram as your Language of Value, these three styles can illuminate the pathways that will move us forward from flared tempers and bad feelings to optimal resolution.

While we would each benefit by becoming fluent in all three styles, it's helpful to know which of these styles you tend to favor. And as you get to know your team members, you'll learn which style they need to experience reconciliation as well. So let's dig in:

Emotional Realness

People who default to this style don't truly feel that conflict is resolved until the other person understands the emotional impact of the conflict. The emotions may be focused on how they experienced the inciting incident or debate, or they may be more about how they felt as the conflict was happening.

This conflict style is a great starting place when we are trying to repair relationships because it highlights the **need for empathy**. Those of us who favor the other two styles tend to rush past empathy, which can feel dismissive to the person with whom we're in conflict. In rushing, we send a message that says, "It happened. Get over it and move on."

Unfortunately, those on your team who are best suited to this style probably won't be able to move on until you really listen to how the situation felt to them, letting them tell their own story about what happened. After hearing that story in full, you can apologize or clarify with authenticity and empathy.

Once we've listened fully, we're still going to need the other two styles.

Competency

People who default to this style cannot truly move on from conflict until both parties have agreed on how this situation will be addressed in the future. How do the tasks, methods, or expectations have to change to avoid dealing with this particular problem again? How does the way they engaged the conflict itself need to change? They want clear, actionable steps.

When we're working on repair, this is a crucial step

because it addresses **the need for a solution.** But those of us who favor the other two styles may want to skip the solution step, which will infuriate our friends and colleagues with a competency bent. "How can you say you're sorry with no plan to address this pattern in the future?" they might ask.

If we truly want to extract the intelligence available to us in conflict, we have to include this style. We can look backward and get real about where harm has been done, and that will grow our empathy. But that empathy turns into strategy when it helps us formulate a stronger path forward.

This is where wisdom comes in.

Positive Outlook

This last style addresses **the need to return to a positive relationship**. If you think of conflict as a relational withdrawal, then it's important to make some new deposits, so to speak, in order to get back to good standing.

In corporate spaces, this element of conflict resolution is sometimes ignored or looked at as superfluous. "The conflict is resolved—now do your job."

Too often we practice empathy and strategy, and then we walk away from the table. We've done the repair, but the conflict lingers. Yes, it's been put to bed, but what do you say to that person when you run into them in the break room tomorrow morning? How do you know when you've gotten back to good?

People who lead with this style tend to do this without even thinking. When the connection feels bad, they work hard to create moments of positive interaction in the wake of conflict. The danger, of course, is that when they do this before they've shown empathy or increased competence, it can ring a bit hollow. Which is why this is an important style, but jumping straight to it can cause its own harm.

So Now What?

If you are in relationships with humans, which we all are, you will experience conflict. If you manage humans, their conflict will become your conflict. So, what can you do with this information to make life easier?

First, know your own style. If none of these immediately rang a bell of recognition, spend the next week observing yourself whenever you need to resolve relational tension. Perhaps you made a small mistake that irritated your supervisor or flew into a rage with someone when a project went sideways.

Or maybe you came home from a long day at work and snapped at your 12-year-old because you just could not take another minute of Minecraft storytelling. (Just us? Cool, cool.).

Whatever it is, take the opportunity to self-observe

and determine what your instinct is when you're ready to do some damage control.

Second, get curious about the people around you. Observe all of them—your supervisor, teammates, direct reports, family members, neighbors, and friends. If you care about them, getting curious will help.

If you're trying to repair harm, and it doesn't seem to be working, let that be a sign: This may not be their Conflict Resolution Style. It may be time to switch gears. And for your most important connections, it may be worth some candid conversation.

Ask questions about their style. You might say, "What would help you feel like this conflict is truly resolved?" or "Would it help if we agreed to some guard rails going forward?"

And of course, we want this information to flow in both directions, so share your own Conflict Resolution Style. For example, you might say, "I know you're trying to come up with a solution, and I appreciate that, but I really just need you to hear my experience first. Can we problem solve once I feel you understand what I felt in that moment?"

With these elements in mind, not only will you be on your way back to good a lot quicker, but you'll also feel more freedom to collaborate and debate because you know that repair is possible—and there's a lot of safety and confidence in that!

Things to Remember:

- After conflict, if your working relationship is going to continue, repair must occur.
- Everyone has a Conflict Resolution Style preference—start by knowing your own, then get curious about the people around you.
- Even though everyone has a preferred Conflict Resolution Style, it's important to go through all three for solid repair.

REFLECT

1. What stands out to you from this chapter?

REFLECT

2. How will you put this into action to improve your own collaboration skills?

REFLECT

3. How will you utilize this with your team, family, or community?

ADDITIONAL NOTES

EPILOGUE: WHY WE DO THIS WORK

People often ask us, "What makes you want to do this kind of work?" And they generally follow it with some variation of, "It would make me so anxious!"

For us the answer is simple: We love being part of a process that makes people happier.

As Americans, we spend an estimated 90,000 hours of our lifetimes at work, and we don't want each workday to drain our life force like some kind of psychic vampire.

We decided years ago that we wanted most of those hours to leave us feeling satisfied and proud. We think it's possible to build a life in which we look forward to going to work, spending time with people we enjoy, people who value us—all while also hitting our goals and KPIs out of the park!

We're glad you've made it all the way to this epilogue, and we hope that means we've provided some valuable takeaways. But you're not done yet!

Now, it's time to make a choice.

You and your team can continue to get the same results you always have, putting the "Hope Strategy" into play (click your heels three times, and just hope that everything on your team gets better). Or you can *invest* in making things better.

We'll consider our investment in this book successful if the ideas we've shared have started to take root in you already, and you plan to start approaching team collaboration a little differently. It's time to make room for *communal intelligence*—and even *conflict*—and to step into these spaces with more positive vibes (We can all improve on the classic, "Oh @#$! Here we go again.").

If you'd like to accelerate your team approach to collaboration and conflict, visit us at **https://kimberlyandcoach.com**, or email us directly at **coach@kimberlyandcoach.com**[22]. Drop us a line and tell us what's going on! In response, **we'd love to share two or three ideas to help your team move from chaos to collaboration.**

Thanks for hanging out with us! We'd love to see you IRL (In Real Life, as the gamers say) sometime soon!

Cheers!

Kimberly and Coach
Your Friendly Neighborhood
Team Dynamics Consultants and Speakers

END NOTES

---

[1] You'll find a good explanation of "Mini-Me" here: https://en.wikipedia.org/wiki/Mini-Me
But if you're not familiar with the classic Austin Powers films that highlight this concept, it's worth a Friday or Saturday night to educate yourself. Go ahead, order a pizza or your favorite takeout, and catch *Austin Powers: The Spy Who Shagged Me* and *Goldmember.*

[2] Okay, maybe some flute enthusiast out there would like that. But we weren't able to find any references to a flutes-only symphonic work—so, just go with us on this.

[3] Have we used the Sorting Hat tool in a professional context? No, not yet. But it's undeniably fun. Here's a scientifically validated quiz to help you get sorted:

https://time.com/4809884/harry-potter-house-sorting-hat-quiz/.
Yes, Kimberly and Coach both came up as Gryffindor.

[4] You can catch a quick synopsis and why we love each of these tools in Appendix A at the end of this book.

[5]https://www.fastcompany.com/90716245/sinking-1000-nyc-subway-cars-in-the-atlantic-to-create-a-reef-didnt-go-as-planned.

[6]https://www.nature.org/en-us/what-we-do/our-priorities/provide-food-and-water-sustainably/food-and-water-stories/global-fisheries/.

[7] Listen, people argue with us all the time about the validity of these tools because they read an article somewhere. But we're not talking about the ASVAB (a test used by the military to place people into specialized jobs) here. People who argue about these tools are usually not trying to build out collaboration, they're trying to establish a command-and-control taxonomy to categorize and pigeon-hole employees, rather than humanize the workplace. These tools need to be kept in their proper place.

[8]https://www.discovermagazine.com/mind/how-learning-a-language-changes-your-brain.

[9]https://knowledge.wharton.upenn.edu/article/microsofts-ceo-on-how-empathy-sparks-innovation/.

[10] See https://en.wikipedia.org/wiki/Redbird_Reef.

[11] We're sure that some consultants were paid large sums of money to create said documents. As consultants ourselves, we throw no shade ☺, we just prefer when values take root and stay in the conversation.

[12] This may be a shocking truth to some readers, but 10 people, 100,000 people, or even 1,000,000 people really can be wrong, even though advertisers use this kind of logical fallacy ALL THE FREAKING TIME. It just makes us shake our heads that WE STILL FALL FOR IT in the 21st century. BTW, the logical fallacy is called Appeal to Popularity, and you can learn more about it here: https://en.wikipedia.org/wiki/Argumentum_ad_popu-lum.

[13]https://www.gallup.com/workplace/391922/em-ployee-engagement-slump-continues.aspx

[14] "Oof" is now an actual documented word according to Merriam-Webster. No, really, it is. See: https://www.mer-riam-webster.com/dictionary/oof

[15]https://en.wikipedia.org/wiki/Law-yers,_Guns_and_Money.

[16]https://en.wikipedia.org/wiki/Food_desert.

[17] The False Dilemma is a common logical fallacy used by motivational speakers and political despots alike,

and while sometimes either-or is an actual scenario, it's not as common. Other options often are available, even if they're not easily seen. See https://en.wikipedia.org/wiki/False_dilemma.

[18]Things That Make You Go Hmmm was a song and quote from the 1990's https://en.wikipedia.org/wiki/Things_That_Make_You_Go_Hmmm...

[19] The Smurfs were a popular 1980s cartoon on Saturday mornings. https://www.youtube.com/watch?v=0QjFt72__XA

[20] For those who were not children of the 1980s, Voltron was a cartoon and toy series in which five robot lions transformed and combined to create one powerful robot. See https://en.wikipedia.org/wiki/Voltron and https://youtu.be/3HgWCp79nzI

[21] DACI is a decision making framework we have often used with clients to help structure healthy debate, and also to bring clarity to a variety of points of decision. See https://www.atlassian.com/team-playbook/plays/daci.

[22] Coach will always answer your emails faster than Kimberly. He's a nerd like that. Kimberly—well, she has other great qualities.

ABOUT THE AUTHORS

Kimberly & Coach help organizations turn chaos into collaboration by transforming ordinary teams into extraordinary powerhouses. Through professional development, keynote speaking, leadership labs, coaching clinics, executive coaching, and team retreats, they bring new insights about culture, team dynamics, and collective intelligence to leaders and businesses around the world.

Kimberly consults with companies of all sizes, from small regional teams and startups to large international organizations. Her collaborations as a team dynamics consultant and practitioner have resulted in millions of dollars saved, numerous conflicts resolved, and marked increases in employee engagement and retention. CEOs and managers report fewer sleepless nights and worried mornings, and employees all over the globe have said they are enjoying their work and their teams—and that's good news!

Coach has worked in technology for 20+ years with the military, government agencies, and corporations of all sizes. He speaks tech and team dynamics with equal ease, and his work in tech education has reached around the world, from Ohio to Switzerland to NASA headquarters. As a team dynamics consultant and practitioner, he takes the worst-case behaviors he's seen firsthand in a variety of industries and transforms them into best practices that enhance both management and team members' performance and well-being.

Kimberly and Coach are both MPACT Certified coaches, and they've been mentored by the likes of Les Brown and David Newman. They have been working together to elevate teams since 2016, but they've been married since 2001. They live in Austin, Texas, with their son Jack, Kimberly's mother Peggie, and rescue dog Captain O'ccino.

APPENDIX A: A FEW OF OUR FAVORITE LANGUAGE OF VALUE TOOLS

MPACT

From the MPACT Website

"Every leader wants to lead a team that's making a meaningful impact. The problem is that few leaders have access to the practical tools they need to help their people thrive.

MPACT exists because we believe everyone deserves to be part of a flourishing team that's making an impact. That's why we developed an assessment and practical framework that helps leaders unlock the potential inside their teams."

Website

https://www.mpactq.com/

Cost

$49

Why We Love It

The MPACT assessment has a fantastic visual interface and great team tools. It's fast and simple enough on the surface to get team members insights into their preferences on how they elevate and collaborate with others, but there's a deeper level of data that can be used to get further insights. Acclimating team members is easy, with fast 2-minute videos to introduce them to the highlights of their MPACT profile.

Kimberly & Coach are both MPACT Certified Coaches and actively use this tool with their most successful clients

VAK Assessment

This Language of Value identifies each team member's primary and secondary learning style. It is primarily used to improve communication, training, and marketing by considering additional communication routes.

Website

http://www.educationplanner.org/students/self-assessments/learning-styles.shtml

Cost

Free

Why We Love It

Identifying team members' information processing preferences can bring quick wins around differences in communication styles. It can provide immediate insights into miscommunications. The VAK can be used in large meetings and we highlight it often in our interactive keynote talks to get folks tuned into the usefulness of a Language of Value.

CliftonStrengths (Formally StrengthsFinder) From the Gallup Website

"You know your team members better than anyone. But do you know *why* they do what they do, *what* motivates them or *when* they're at their best? We make it easy to find out. When you and your team use the

CliftonStrengths assessment to discover what you do best, you'll have stronger team dynamics, better conversations and increased collaboration."

Website

https://www.gallup.com/cliftonstrengths/en/252137/home.aspx

Cost

$19-$59

Why We Love It

CliftonStrengths is wildly positive, and has a fantastic depth of strengths that bring a very well-rounded picture of individual capabilities. For teams that are operating under heavy negativity, this tool can lighten the emotional environment. Not to mention, it's backed by Gallup's world class data analysis!

Enneagram

This Language of Value identifies each team member's "Type" to understand their key values, desires, fears, and strengths. It's excellent for increasing understanding around how people make decisions and respond to stress, recognizing and short-circuiting unhealthy patterns, and pursuing growth toward healthier interaction. Teams can be mapped on the enneagram circle, or in various triads.

Website
https://www.enneagraminstitute.com/
Cost
$12

Why We Love It

The enneagram is a narrative tradition that provides a deep dive into reactivity and default modes of action. It's a great tool in high trust environments, and has a wide acceptance in many spiritual traditions. It's especially useful in churches, temples, mosques, and organizations that have a spiritual or personal development bent.

----

16 Personalities (Myers-Briggs)

From the website: "In our free type descriptions you'll learn what really drives, inspires, and worries different personality types, helping you build more meaningful relationships. Understand your team better with our Team Assessments. Improve communication, create harmony, and help team members develop their individual strengths. Works for teams of all sizes."

Website
https://www.16personalities.com/
Cost
Free, with advanced options up to $169

Why We Love It

Myers-Briggs is one of the most well-known tools available, and there are a lot of supporting materials and resources available for it. Many team members may already have some knowledge of Myers-Briggs from school or past jobs, so adoption can sometimes be easier.

APPENDIX B: CHOOSE YOUR LANGUAGE OF VALUE TOOL

Instructions: Consider where your team would fall on each of the following poles, and place an X on each line. Be as honest as you can. Then look over your marks and consider which of the tools may best fit your team's needs.

Key:

MPACT—MPACT Assessment

CS –CliftonStrengths

MB—Myers-Briggs

ENN—Enneagram

VAK—Visual-Auditory-Kinesthetic

How well does my team communicate?

Miscommunication   Easy Communication

VAK   MPACT   MB   ENN, CS

How much do team members trust each other?

Low Trust   High Trust

VAK MPACT   CS   MB   ENN

Do we have a problem with negativity?

Team Leans Negative   Team Leans Positive

CS MPACT   VAK   MB   ENN

How long have we been together?

Brand-New Team   Well-Established Team

VAK, CS, MPACT   MB   ENN

How relational is my team?

Professional Distance   Friendship Environment

VAK   MPACT   CS   MB   ENN

How often do we see each other in person?

Virtual Team   In-Person Team

VAK   MPACT   CS   MB ENN

Is Cost a Factor?

Needs to be Free   Willing to Invest

VAK/MB   ENN   CS   MPACT

Is simplicity a priority?

Simplicity, please   Complexity is A-Okay

VAK, MPACT   MB   CS   ENN

> **Which of the tools might be candidates for your company's Language of Value?**

For a free 15-minute conversation about your team and this tool, visit https://kimberlyandcoach.com or just email coach@kimberlyandcoach.com